Worms

by Theresa Greenaway

Photographs by Chris Fairclough

WAYLAND

Minibeast Pets

Caterpillars   Spiders
Slugs and Snails   Worms

Cover photograph: An earthworm pulling
a dead leaf down into its burrow.

All Wayland books encourage
children to read and help them improve their literacy.

✓ The contents page, page numbers, headings, diagrams and index help locate specific pieces of information.

✓ The glossary reinforces alphabetic knowledge and extends vocabulary.

✓ On page 30 you can find out about other books and videos dealing with the same subject.

© Copyright 1999 (text) Wayland Publishers Limited
61 Western Road, Hove, East Sussex BN3 1JD

Planned and produced by Discovery Books Limited
Project Editors: Gianna Williams, Kathy DeVico
Project Manager: Joyce Spicer
Illustrated by Jim Chanell and Stefan Chabluk
Designed by Ian Winton

British Library Cataloguing in Publication Data
Greenaway, Theresa, 1947-
  Worms. – (Minibeast Pets)
  1. Worms – Juvenile literature
  2. Invertebrates as pets – Juvenile literature
  I. Title
  592.3
HARDBACK   ISBN 0 7502 2510 6
PAPERBACK   ISBN 0 7502 2514 9
Printed and bound in the USA

Find Wayland on the Internet at http://www.wayland.co.uk

Contents

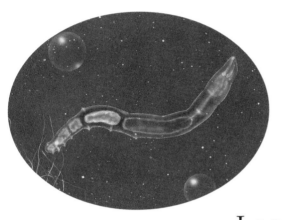

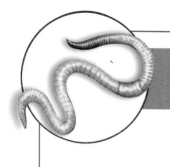

Keeping worms

Did you know there are more than a million different kinds of worm? They can be found in all sorts of places, not just in the soil, but in seas and oceans, too.

Not many people know exactly how worms live, so keeping them as pets is a good way to find out more.

A worm's body is divided into rings called segments. Each segment has bristles which help it to move.

◄ Worms move slowly, so when you find one, take a good look at it before it slithers away.

Worms produce a slimy mucus all over their skin. This helps them slide through the soil. It also stops them getting too dry. If worms become too dry they will die.

▼ This is what earthworm bristles look like, seen through a magnifying glass.

Worms have no eyes and no antennae, but they do have a mouth. Watch to see in which direction a worm moves. Then you will know which is the front end.

Always wash your hands after handling worms.

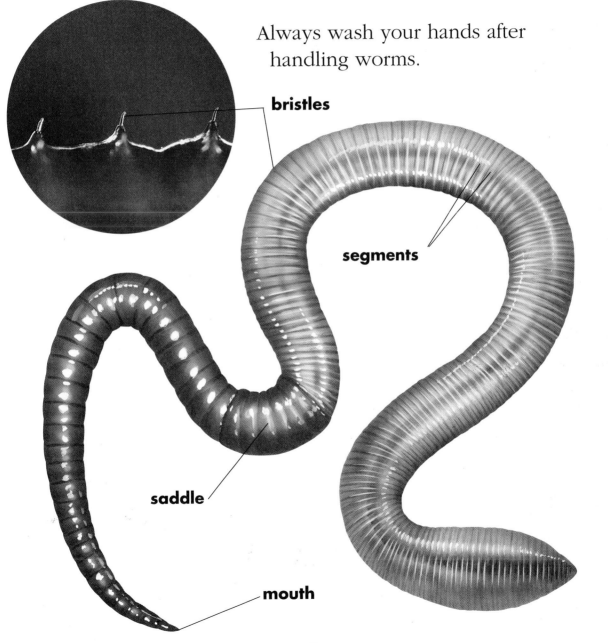

bristles

segments

saddle

mouth

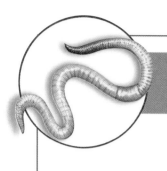

Finding worms

In mild weather, most worms live near the top of the soil. They burrow through the earth finding things to eat.

Small worms often live among the moist litter of fallen leaves in wooded areas.

Worms that swim

Bristle worms are relatives of earthworms, but they live in the sea. Although it is beautiful, this bristle worm is poisonous.

Worms like damp soil, but most of them do not like soil that is always too wet. On a rainy night, worms often leave their burrows. They crawl around on the surface looking for fallen leaves.

Look under stones, flowerpots or logs. You will also find lots of worms in compost heaps.

▼ Sludge worms like smelly mud at the bottom of ponds. They have red blood, which shows through their thin skin.

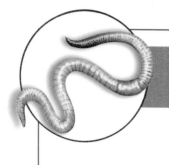

Worm collecting

First find some jars or plastic containers for your worms.

If you do not want to touch them, take a big plastic scoop with you. Remember that worms have soft bodies, so you must handle them gently.

Using a trowel or small spade, dig into the soil until you uncover a worm. Dig slowly, or you might slice one in half! Pick the worm up carefully, and put it into a jar with a little soil. Write on a label where you found the worm and how deep down it was.

Put a lid with air holes on the jar.

Make sure you put your containers in the shade
if you are searching for more worms.

Heaps of worms

If you have a compost heap in your garden, carefully turn some of it over.
Sometimes you will find hundreds of brandling worms writhing around.
Scoop some into a plastic container with a spoonful of wet compost.

Identifying worms

Most worms are known simply as 'earthworms', but there are many different kinds.

Worms may be different colours and different sizes. Write down in a notebook where each one was found, what kind of soil it was living in and its colour. Using a plastic ruler, try to measure the length of each worm.

Don't worry if you are not able to tell one from another. It is quite difficult.

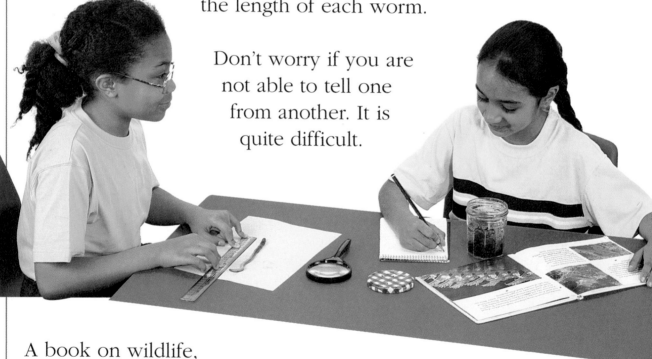

A book on wildlife, or a visit to a natural history museum, may help you identify your worms.

Marine worms have segments, just like earthworms, but they do not look like their earthworm relatives.

Some have lots of long bristles, or are covered in little coloured scales. Others look almost hairy.

▲ Green paddle worms live in rock pools at the edge of the sea.

Giant worms

The giant earthworm can grow to a length of over 3 metres! It is the world's biggest earthworm and is found in Australia.

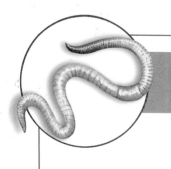

Homes for worms

Make homes for your worms that are as similar as possible to the places where you found them. If you found the worms on a lawn, dig up some small tufts of grass to put in their new home.

You will need a tall narrow glass or plastic container. Put in layers of leaf litter and crumbly soil, or compost, and a layer of sand. The total depth of leaves, soil and sand should be about 20 cm.

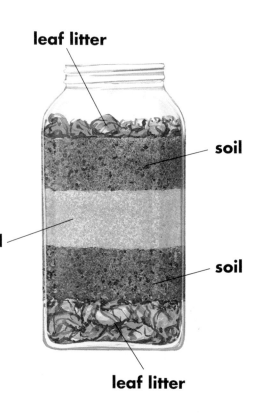

leaf litter

soil

sand

soil

leaf litter

Spread some damp, fallen leaves over the surface.

Sprinkle some water over the leaves and soil. Then place your worms on top and watch how they burrow.

Cover your wormery with black paper or cloth, or keep it inside a dark box. Worms stay hidden most of the time. If they come out during the day, there is a danger that they will dry up and die.

A house of sand

A marine worm called the sand mason oozes sticky mucus out of its skin. It makes its home by cementing sand and tiny fragments of shell onto this mucus.

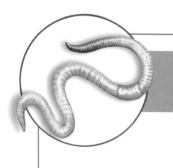

Looking after worms

Worms do not like their homes to get too hot, too dry, or too wet. As you collect your worms, feel the soil they are in. It is probably crumbly and moist.

Try to keep the soil in your worm's home the same.

If you keep your worms outside, make sure they are sheltered from rain or they might drown.

If the soil gets too dry and hard, the worms will not be able to tunnel through it.

Although worms do not fight, do not put too many in each container. They will become overcrowded.

Safe from enemies, worms can live for up to ten years. But in the wild their lives are usually much shorter, as birds, foxes, shrews and moles love to eat them.

Worms in danger
Birds can hear worms moving along their burrows. If a bird pecks the head or tail off an earthworm, it can grow a new one. But worms that are cut in half cannot make two new worms – both halves die.

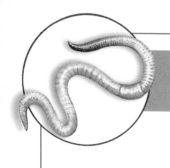

Feeding worms

Most worms eat the bits of dead leaves and plants that are found in soil. They also feed on the tiny creatures, fungi and bacteria that live in the soil.

The worm swallows mud as it tunnels. All the food is digested as the mud goes through the worm's belly.

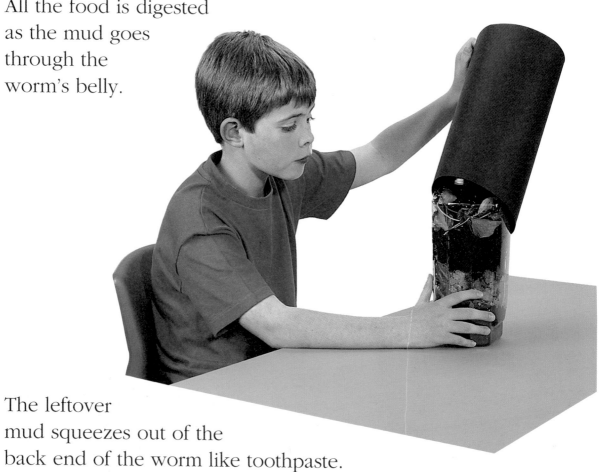

The leftover mud squeezes out of the back end of the worm like toothpaste.

Some earthworms squirt the mud they swallow into a little pile on the surface of the ground. These piles are called worm casts.

Worms often pull dead leaves into the entrances of their burrows. Then they can feed in safety underground.

▶ A leaf at the top of an earthworm's burrow keeps it safe from the probing beaks of birds.

Meat-eaters

Many worms eat the little bits of dead animals that are in the soil they swallow. But some kinds, like this chaetogaster, eat other tiny creatures or their eggs.

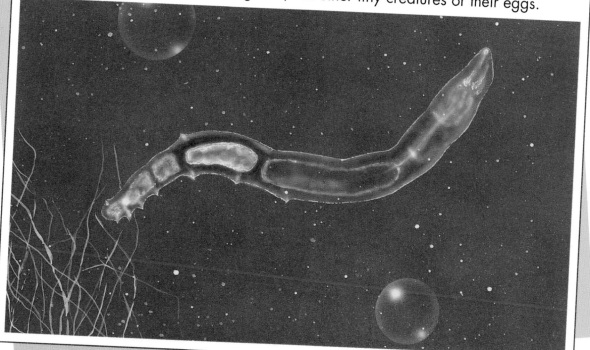

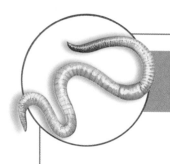

Worm-watching

If you keep your worms in a clear container, you may be able to see the tunnels that they make through the soil.

Watch how your worms move. Because they have layers of muscle just under their skin, worms can stretch out until they are very long and thin. They can also squash up until they are short and fat. Worms can even be thin in one part of their bodies and fat in another at the same time.

There are four pairs of bristles on the lower half of every segment of a worm's body. These help the worm grip onto the soil to try to keep birds from pulling it out.

A worm's bristles also help it shoot back into its burrow if danger threatens.

▶ Pick up a large worm and hold it in your hand. Very gently, stroke the worm from back to front along the lower half of its body. You will be able to feel its tiny bristles.

How worms move

Worms move along their tunnels by stretching the front part of their bodies. Then they grip the sides with their tiny bristles and pull up the back part.

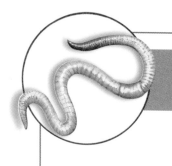

Reproduction

A worm is both male and female, but worms still have to pair up in order to make eggs.

A grown-up worm's body has a thick band around it called the saddle. After a pair of worms have mated, they separate. The saddle of each worm oozes out a collar-like ring of mucus, in which the worm lays eggs. Then the worm wriggles out of this ring, which seals up and hardens into a cocoon.

Hatching

Earthworms bury their cocoons in the soil. There may be up to 20 eggs in each cocoon, but only one or two usually hatch out. The other eggs provide food for the little worms while they are in the cocoon.

Worm eggs take between one and five months to hatch. Each hatchling looks like a tiny adult worm.

You may be able to watch worms mating. Go into your garden on a warm, damp evening. Worms like darkness, so tape some red cellophane over your torch.

▲ Some worms mate underground, but others come out of their burrows to find a mate.

Hot and cold

When the top layer of soil starts to get too cold in the winter, or too warm and dry in the summer, worms tunnel down into the earth. This is because extreme heat or cold cannot reach deep into the soil. Worms may go one metre below the surface.

▼ In very cold weather, some worms coil up at the bottom of their tunnels and rest.

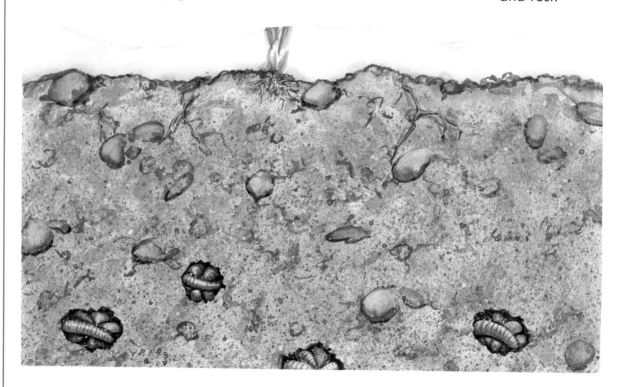

Earthworms have no noses, but they do need to breathe. When they are deep in the ground, they take oxygen into their blood through their thin skin.

A lugworm is a kind of bristle worm that lives on muddy or sandy beaches. It makes a large, U-shaped burrow that stretches 25 cm down into the wet sand.

Some bristle worms swim in the shallow water of rock pools and hide under stones to keep cool.

▲ Lugworm casts on the seashore. Lugworms stay cool in their burrows below the sand when the tide goes out.

Feather-duster worms

These marine worms live buried in chalky tubes attached to rocks or shipwrecks. They stick a crown of gills (breathing organs) out into the water. These sweep tiny plankton, little bits of seaweed and sea creatures into their mouths.

Keeping a record

Why not make a scrapbook about your worms?
Record the date you collected them, and where
you found them. Every time you notice something
interesting about your worms, make notes and
drawings.

EARTHWORM

Found: On the grass
Date: 2 September
I found this worm on a rainy
afternoon. It is 10 centimetres
long when it stretches out.

This is a photo
of a worm cast
in my garden.

The Latin name for worm is
Lumbricus terrestris.

If you find pictures of worms in magazines, paste them
in your scrapbook, too. Try to find out more about your
worms from books or computer programs.

The activity of worms is very helpful to farmers and gardeners.

Worm tunnels allow air to reach the roots of plants. Also, the way worms eat mud in one place and squirt it out in another mixes up the soil. These worm activities help plants to grow.

Small but useful

The famous scientist Charles Darwin studied worms. He worked out that certain kinds of worms could produce about 10 tonnes of worm casts on the surface of just half a hectare of meadow every year!

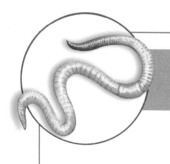

Letting them go

When you let your worms
go, take each worm
back to the place
you found it.

Choose a mild, damp evening. Gently tip your worms
out of their container onto the ground. Make sure they
are hidden by leaves, or carefully place a piece of wood
over them so they can burrow into the ground safely.

Put lugworms, and other bristle worms that you find by the sea, in a pan of fresh sea water while you watch them. Do not keep them for long – they need lots of fresh sea water or they will die. An hour or two is long enough to look closely at them, especially if you have a magnifying glass.

Remember to pour them back where you found them.

The great escape

If moles find more worms than they can eat, they bite off their heads to stop them wriggling away. Then they save them for later. But if they leave them for too long, the worms can grow new heads and escape!

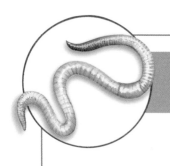

Amazing worms

Christmas tree worms live inside small, chalky tubes attached to corals. When they feed, they put out pairs of brightly-coloured tentacles that look very much like little Christmas trees.

▼ These worms have tentacles which look just like tiny, brightly-lit Christmas trees.

Honeycomb worms live in groups on rocks close to the shore. Each worm builds a tube by cementing grains of sand together. These tubes make a honeycomb pattern all over the rocks.

The peacock worm makes a tube by sticking little bits of sand and mud together with mucus. The tube may be up to 20 cm long.

When it feeds, the worm sticks a fan of feathery gills out into the sea. These draw little pieces of food down into its mouth, which is in the centre of the fan.

The gills also help it to breathe, by taking in oxygen from the sea water.

▲ These peacock worms will pull their gills back into their tubes in times of danger.

Velvet worms have many pairs of legs and crawl rather like caterpillars. They live in the rain forests of Central America.

Fireworms live inside the sponges on which they feed. When they want to mate, the females swim to the sea's surface and make a glowing light. Males make flashing lights, and swim towards the steadily glowing females.

Finding out more

BOOKS

My Best Book of Creepy Crawlies by Claire Llewellyn (Kingfisher, 1998)

Put Something Beastly in Your Pocket: Worm by S.Wiseman (Bookmart, 1996)

The Really Horrible Horny Toad (and other cold, clammy creatures) by T. Greenaway (Dorling Kindersley, 1998)

Topic Box: Minibeasts by Sally Morgan (Wayland, 1995)

Wings, Stings and Wriggly Things: Minibeasts by M. Jenkins (Walker, 1996)

VIDEOS

Amazing Animals: Minibeasts (Dorling Kindersley, 1996)

Amazing Animals: Creepy Crawly Animals (Dorling Kindersley, 1999)

See How They Grow: Minibeasts (Dorling Kindersley, 1992)

FURTHER INFORMATION

CLEAPPS School Science Service will be able to help with any aspect of keeping minibeasts.   Tel: 01895 251496

SCIENCE
Observing minibeasts
Animal classification / variation
Animal habitats
Life cycles
Life processes
Moving and growing
Food chains / nutrition
Animal adaptations
Animal behaviour
Use of magnifying glass

ENGLISH
Following instructions
Recording observations
Using glossaries
Extending scientific vocabulary
Research skills

ART, DESIGN & TECHNOLOGY
Close observation: drawings of minibeasts
Investigating camouflage / mimicry
Designing and making (scrapbooks, containers for minibeasts)

Minibeast Pets TOPIC WEB

MATHS
Measuring skills
Collecting and recording data

GEOGRAPHY
The seasons
Weather and climate

PHSE
Caring for living things
Showing respect
Taking responsibility

Glossary

antennae The feelers that some small creatures have on their heads, which help them to 'taste' and smell.

bacteria Very tiny living organisms.

cocoon An outer case that protects the delicate eggs of earthworms.

compost heap A mound of grass cuttings, vegetable peelings, leaves and dead plants, piled up in a heap outside and left to rot.

fungi A large group of living organisms, many of which produce mushrooms and toadstools.

gills Very thin-skinned organs that help many water animals to breathe. They take in dissolved oxygen from water.

identify To find out the name of something.

leaf litter A layer of fallen leaves, mostly from trees.

marine To do with the sea.

mating The coming together of a male and female animal in order to produce young.

mucus A slimy liquid produced over the surface of a worm's skin, which keeps it from drying up.

organisms Living things.

plankton Tiny plants and animals that swim or float near the surface of the sea.

saddle A band of thick skin around an earthworm that oozes out a special thick collar of mucus.

Index

The publishers would like to thank the following for their permission to reproduce photographs:
cover Kathie Atkinson/Oxford Scientific Films, 4 Johan De Meester/Oxford Scientific Films, 5 David Thompson/Oxford Scientific Films, 6 Michael Glover/Bruce Coleman, 7 G. I. Bernard/Oxford Scientific Films, 9 Kim Taylor/Bruce Coleman, 11 top G. I. Bernard/Oxford Scientific Films, 11 bottom A.N.T/Natural History Photographic Agency, 13 Rodger Jackman/Oxford Scientific Films, 15 Kim Taylor/Bruce Coleman, 17 Kathie Atkinson/Oxford Scientific Films, 20 David Thompson/Oxford Scientific Films, 21 David T. Grewock/Frank Lane Picture Agency, 23 top Eckart Pott/Bruce Coleman, 23 bottom Paul Kay/Oxford Scientific Films, 27 David Thompson/Oxford Scientific Films, 28 Ian Cartwright/Frank LanePicture Agency, 29 D. P. Wilson/Frank Lane Picture Agency.